The Good Shepherd!

"JESUS in 100 Ways" Series

Papa & Mama Goose

The Good Shepherd!
"JESUS in 100 Ways" Series

Papa & Mama Goose

Copyright © 2020
Enchanted Rose Publishing
P.O. Box 991
Hempstead, TX 77445

Published by Enchanted Rose Publishing
Layout by Cynthia D. Johnson @
www.diverseskillscenter.com

Written by Papa & Mama Goose

Printed in the United States of America
ISBN-13: 978-1-947799-69-1

I'm like a little lamb when troubles come to me.

I do not think of fighting, I only want to flee!

I flee to JESUS!

I flee to JESUS!

I mix my directions, and often lose
my way...

My Savior is before me and bids me not to stray.

I follow JESUS!

I follow JESUS!

When grazing across uneven fields, sometimes my legs get stuck...

As tears begin to fill my eyes,
my Good Shepherd picks me up.

I cry to JESUS!

I cry to JESUS!

When many troubles crowd my mind, and peace has let me go...

You gently wrap me around your neck and carry my heavy load.

JESUS carries me!

JESUS carries me!

**When we've had our share of food
and making a lot of noise...**

We run like a herd of cattle when we hear our Shepherd's voice!

We follow JESUS!

We follow JESUS!

The Good Shepherd!

"JESUS in 100 Ways" Series

Written by Papa & Mama Goose

Copyright 2020

by

Mama Goose Books

Hempstead, Texas

Papa & Mama Goose Media

Through the power of their faith and instructions from GOD's HOLY SPIRIT, these humble servants of CHRIST take us back to our beginning...The Bible. Although Papa and Mama Goose have written a plethora of books, none can hold a candle to how the WORD of GOD has guided their lives. Realizing that life on Earth is temporal, Papa and Mama Goose wanted to write Books about the Bible that would provide a Biblical Foundation for young children. The goal of the books is to teach youngsters to know and fall deeply in Love with GOD.

It was during their years in college that Papa and Mama Goose found CHRIST. They were taught the Gospel and baptized into the Prairie View CHURCH of CHRIST at Prairie View A & M University in Prairie View, Texas. Papa and Mama Goose enjoy sharing the same spiritual birthday. Currently, the dynamic duo are faithful members of the Fifth Ward CHURCH of CHRIST in Houston, Texas.

Follow Me On…

 Facebook

www.facebook.com/gomamagoose

 Twitter

@GoMamaGoose

 Instagram

MamaGoose Paris

gomamagoose@gmail.com

www.ingramcontent.com/pod-product-compliance
Lightning Source LLC
Chambersburg PA
CBHW041241040426

42445CB00004B/107